The Science of Vehicles

The Turbo-Charged Truth About Trucks and Cars

Written by
Roger Canavan

BOOK HOUSE
a SALARIYA imprint

Contents

Introduction

Look at any busy city street and you'll see a big collection of cars and trucks. You've probably ridden many times in some of them – passenger cars, school buses or taxis. But sharing road space with those are delivery vans, fuel trucks and emergency vehicles. And outside cities you'll find farm vehicles, giant construction trucks and even cars that seem more like boats or planes. This book looks at the science that lies behind that wide range of cars and trucks. You'll see how some of the same scientific principles that you learn in the classroom – with terms like force, energy and motion – are at work with these vehicles. Whether it's petrol engines powered with timed explosions, electric vehicles that run on batteries, or rocket-like high-speed cars with sleek shapes, it's science that makes all of them go.

Drivers of 'horseless carriages' in many countries had to have someone walk in front with a red flag to warn pedestrians and horses of the approaching vehicle.

Paving the way

The breakthroughs of the Industrial Revolution meant that people could harness new types of power. And it wasn't long before engineers and inventors were testing these new technologies to find better – and faster – ways of transporting people and goods. By the end of the nineteenth century, the technology known as internal combustion had become dominant. Petrol-powered vehicles signalled the end of the age of the horse. Engineers and inventors saw the potential and began finding new ways to produce speed and power – efforts that continue to this day.

End of an era

Horses had provided transport for centuries, and most people were familiar with how far a horse could ride in an hour, or how much farmland a team of horses could plough in a day. Eighteenth-century Scottish engineer James Watt invented the word 'horsepower' to compare the output of steam engines with the power of draft horses – horses that pull heavy loads.

Steam power?

Just as the Industrial Revolution was built on steam power, early designers used steam to 'drive' their cars. The force created by water heated into steam could power machinery. Soon it became clear, though, that steam engines on cars were clumsy and dangerous.

Even today's engineers measure the output of vehicles in 'horsepower' – a throwback to the time when cars were just replacing horses for transport.

New type of fuel

German inventor Karl Benz combined his love of bicycles with his knowledge of trains to produce the first real automobile in 1885. His three-wheeled 'motorwagen' looks spindly to us, but its engine design paved the way for the future. Benz used a mixture of air and petrol (a fuel that burns) to release the energy needed to move the car. This technique, called internal combustion, is still used in most cars.

Fascinating fact

In 1769, more than a century before Benz's Motorwagen, Frenchman Nicolas-Joseph Cugnot developed a steam-powered tractor. This vehicle was heavy and hard to steer. Things got worse for Cugnot two years later when he had the world's first car accident – crashing through a brick wall in Paris and winding up in prison.

Energy transfer

Scientists define energy as 'the ability to do work'. You can't create or destroy energy, but you can store, release or transfer it. The petrol from a filling station has potential energy – energy that's waiting to be used in some way. The spark from the spark plug causes the petrol to burn, which turns it into mechanical energy – which is needed to move the car.

A turbocharger uses the force of the exhaust to power a fan-like device that pumps even more air into the cylinder, allowing it to mix with even more fuel – giving the car more power.

Under the bonnet and beyond

Petrol from a vehicle's fuel tank flows to the engine, where the rhythmic sparks from the spark plugs cause a constant series of mini-explosions. Those explosions – which give the name 'internal combustion' – provide the power.

But that's just the start of a process that has energy constantly being transferred in a car or truck. Ingenious design channels the energy so that the rear (or sometimes front) wheels keep turning – moving the car forwards or backwards.

Got a light?

An electrical signal causes the spark plug in each cylinder to spark, igniting the air and fuel mixture that had been squashed up inside the cylinder. By the time the piston has been pushed down again (because of this mini-explosion), then up again (getting rid of the exhaust), then down again (sucking in more air and fuel), then back up (compression) – it's ready to spark again.

Threads
Centre electrode
Terminal
Insulator
Ground electrode

Going for a spin

Wheels
Engine
Axle
Driveshaft
Differential

The up-down motion of the pistons causes a long driveshaft (connected to the rear axle) to spin. There it meets a gear called a differential, which transfers the spinning motion so that the wheels roll forward or backward, and not sideways.

Front-wheel drive cars don't need a driveshaft because the axle is below the engine. But they still need a differential to turn the direction of the spinning 90 degrees.

How it works

Each piston moves up and down inside one of the engine's metal cylinders. First it moves down, to suck air and fuel into the cylinder. Then it's up again to squeeze that mixture. In the third step, the spark ignites the mixture, pushing the piston down. It moves up again in the last step, pushing exhaust out of the cylinder.

Spark plug

Induction   Compression   Power   Exhaust

Some cities, such as London and Paris, limit the traffic in the centre by forcing drivers to pay an extra charge. The aim is to make traffic move more smoothly and to reduce pollution.

All kinds of cars

Things have changed greatly since the first few cars edged their way along city streets at the breathtaking speed of 8 kph (5 mph). Not only have cars become faster, but they have also become safer, more reliable and more plentiful – with more than a billion in use around the world at last count.

Science is put to work all the time, helping engineers develop cars to cope with steep slopes, freezing temperatures, heavy loads... and rich drivers who demand luxury. Whether a driver wants to drive across the Sahara, commute to work or school comfortably, or deliver flowers to newlyweds, there's a car that suits that job best.

Economy model

'Economy' means the savings in cost to buy – and to run – some cars. Most economy cars are small and light, so they don't need a powerful engine. A smaller engine needs to use less fuel, so the cost is less.

Luxury cars are engineered to provide a smooth ride and almost pure silence inside. Only the super wealthy can afford to buy the most expensive models, which can cost more than a house.

Jeeps

Jeeps were designed as army vehicles able to handle all sorts of roads – or sometimes no roads at all. Their suspension, steering and tyres make them well suited for rough terrain.

Modification

Amateur engineers and mechanics often turn their cars into more powerful or faster versions of the original cars. Modifying the engine, tyres and suspension of a family car can transform it into a racetrack competitor.

Can you believe it?

Some cars have extra features that aren't really scientific – or even necessary. People in the 1950s were fascinated by the first rockets being sent into space. American car designers decided to make cars look more like those rockets. They added enormous 'fins' at the back to look like the fins on rockets. These had nothing to do with the cars' function, but people loved them.

11

Pickup truck

Pickup trucks aren't much bigger than ordinary cars, but their powerful engines and larger storage capacity makes them ideal for transporting goods. Many pickups have four-wheel drive to give them better traction and handling on rough or slippery terrain.

Keep on trucking

The 'workhorses' of the transport world come in all shapes and sizes – each designed to carry out a job in the most scientific way possible. And for trucks, 'scientific' means efficient and secure. Most trucks need large engines to push, pull or carry heavy loads. Speed is less important than the stability to balance cargo or passengers safely and being able to steer and stop safely.

Full load – steady as she goes!

Judging the centre of mass is the important science behind the design of pickup trucks: the weight is balanced between the engine (front axle) and load (over the rear axle).

A car carrier trailer – a truck for transporting cars

Packing a load

Rubbish and recycling trucks are equipped with compactors to let them carry up to six times the volume of uncompacted loads. With so much weight – including the compacting machinery – in the back, they need a third axle for support and grip.

Fascinating fact

Just like bicycles, cars and trucks use gears to climb hills or to save fuel at higher speeds on level roads. Most cars have about five gears. Big trucks need as many as 16 so that the change from one gear to the next is slight. Otherwise the change would put too much strain on the driveshaft.

Bus safety

Passenger safety is the most important engineering feature when designing and building buses. Their great mass distributes the force of any collision. Seats are high, close together and padded so that passengers are protected even if they aren't wearing seat belts.

Many school buses are equipped with routers so that children can connect to the Internet with Wi-Fi. It's ideal for getting a head start on homework if it's a long ride home.

13

First on the scene

Ambulances are fitted with special noise filters so that the loud siren (needed to warn drivers and pedestrians) won't disturb patients inside the ambulance itself.

Emergency vehicles are there when you need them – they have to be. And they rely on a range of scientific and engineering features to do their job. Because emergencies call for urgent responses, these vehicles need to be fast. Police cars are often the most powerful versions of common vehicles such as SUVs and pickup trucks.

Other emergency vehicles resemble vans or trucks, but with special adaptations for their purpose such as firefighting or mountain rescue. It is an engineering challenge to balance these special features with the need to get to and from emergency scenes quickly.

Ambulances

A whole range of engineering and electrical modifications help ambulances travel quickly and smoothly, while retaining contact with hospitals throughout. Special GPS equipment displays the fastest routes, often guiding ambulances up one-way streets in the wrong direction or on pedestrian-only streets.

Firefighting

Fire engines must be able to cope with house fires, wildfires, chemical fires and blazes in city high-rises. Sometimes the team can't predict the type of fire until they arrive, so the truck must carry deluge guns and chemical tanks for electrical and chemical fires as well as the usual pumps, hoses and ladders.

Mountain rescue

Mountain rescue vehicles are specially adapted to cope with steep slopes, deep mud or water, snow and ice... all the while carrying a wide range of rescue and first-aid equipment. Injured hikers or skiers remain secure and stable even as the vehicle crosses the rockiest terrain.

Some city fire engines are equipped with ladders that can extend more than 40 metres (131 feet). The ladders are life savers if people are trapped inside rooms or if an outside fire escape has become unsafe.

Can you believe it?

Weirdly, it seems that the noise made by the sirens on emergency vehicles is not very effective at alerting other drivers. Motorists only tend to notice the noise when the emergency vehicles are very near – and they may not notice at all if they're playing loud music! A recent study found that 90% of drivers' awareness of emergency vehicles was due to visual cues instead – namely, the flashing lights.

15

Henry Ford kept assembly lines rolling – and costs down – by telling customers that they could choose any colour for their Fords, 'as long as it's black'.

The assembly line

America's Ford Motor Company began producing cars on assembly lines in 1913. A rope pulled a chassis along a straight 'assembly line', with 84 teams of workers, each concentrating on one task along the way. The new method reduced assembly time from 12 hours to 90 minutes. It revolutionised how factories – and not just car factories – could work more efficiently.

Roll them out!

The production of automobiles and trucks is one of the most important industries in the world. About 75 million new cars are produced worldwide each year. And just as cars themselves have developed over the years, so too have the ways that they're built. Engineering and technology advances have shaved time and cost from the manufacturing stage. A car, with its 1,800 parts, can now be built in less than a day.

Engineering and technology also play a part in the testing process. No model can go into production until it has passed a series of demanding tests on computer screens, in labs and on tracks outside.

Robots?

Nearly every modern car and truck is produced along an assembly line, but with one big difference compared to the 1913 Ford method. Human beings have been replaced by robots at many stages. Robots can work faster and more accurately than human workers, sometimes for 24 hours a day. China is now building a car factory that will be 'all robot', with no human workers.

Many testing calculations work with the concept of torque, which is a measure of how much force acting on an object causes it to turn.

Test driving

Each new car model is tested over and over again inside factories and on special tracks to measure a wide range of scientific, engineering and safety aspects. Crash tests (with dummies replacing human passengers) measure the effects of impact at different speeds.

Try it yourself

Pinpointing the centre of mass is the key to many car-design tests. You can do your own test using a metre (or yard-) stick and a stone. Balance the stick on two extended fingers, then slide them together slowly – keeping the stick balanced – until they meet. That's the centre of mass. Now try it again, but first have a friend balance a stone at one end of the stick. You'll find that the centre of mass is much closer to the side with the stone.

Chequered flag

Aeroplanes use aerofoils on their wings to provide lift, but the upside-down aerofoils on racing cars help do the opposite – stopping high-speed cars from lifting off the road.

Ever since the first trucks and cars appeared on the scene, people have set up competitions to see which vehicle – or driver – is the fastest. And usually the winner is the one who has put science to use to cross the line first, or fastest.

Many Formula 1 engineering developments eventually find their way into family-car production. Tyre design, aerodynamic (fuel-efficient) body shapes and streamlined gearboxes have all become common.

The appliance of science

Formula 1 manufacturers are constantly tinkering with their designs to get more speed. A typical car can accelerate from 0 to 100 kph (62 mph) in two seconds. During that time it produces more g-forces than a spacecraft launch.

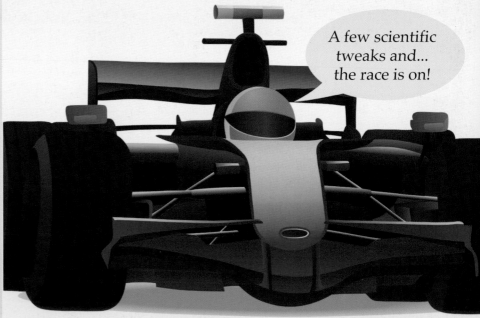

A few scientific tweaks and... the race is on!

Pure speed

Drag racing is some of the fastest – and shortest – car racing around. It's all about acceleration. Some cars reach speeds of 540 kph (335 mph) as they zoom down the 305 metre (1,000 foot) track.

Ice-car racers in Canada and the United States use ordinary cars to race on frozen lakes. Drivers use the science of friction and Newton's Laws of Motion to prevent uncontrolled skids and crashes.

Demolition derby

This crazy event isn't really a race – it's a competition to see which car can survive the most collisions. But some cars can be prepared either to 'give' (absorb force safely) or to bounce away without being badly damaged.

Ouch!

Try it yourself

Fold an A4 sheet of paper so that the short sides meet in the middle. Fold back again (as shown). Lay the paper on a table (as shown) so it forms a tunnel. Blow directly through the tunnel to see how the paper roof gets pushed down. This is exactly how a Formula 1 aerofoil pushes the car down.

1

2

3

Brake lights shine more brightly than the vehicle's other lights to be highly visible in order to alert other drivers to slow down as well.

Controlling Speed

Truck and car designers try to improve the way vehicles can accelerate to help the drivers negotiate traffic and be able to manoeuvre quickly past obstacles. But it's just as important – if not more important – to be able to slow down quickly and safely.

Science plays a leading role in both of these aims. Car designers need to understand the basics about laws of motion in order to prevent dangerous accidents.

Brake improvements

The Anti-lock Braking System (ABS) of most new cars senses when wheels will lock, allowing them to roll more slowly (with more steering control) rather than stopping. Brakes on older cars often locked on slippery surfaces, leading to dangerous skids.

Oh no, I'm skidding!

20

Sensing danger

Brakes are linked to electronic systems that connect many parts of modern cars. Many new cars have electronic sensors that can detect when a pedestrian begins crossing the road – sending a signal to apply the brakes.

Sixty to zero

Many cars are bought because they can move from a stop to about 100 kph (60 mph) super fast – even if drivers will rarely need to accelerate so quickly. But a better option would be to design a car that can go from 60 to 0 quickly and safely, making roads much safer.

64 MPH

The hissing sound when a large truck slows down comes from its air brakes, a system that uses compressed air to apply extra force (friction) to slow the wheels' movement.

Fascinating fact

'Stopping distance' is determined by two main factors. 'Thinking distance' is how far the car travels before the driver reacts by braking.

'Braking distance' is how much further the car goes once the brakes have been hit. Stopping and braking distances increase with speed.

Thinking distance   *Braking distance*   *Stopped*

Unimog

One of the earliest all-terrain vehicles, the Unimog truck, trades off cargo capacity in favour of a flexible frame and high clearance off the ground.

For years, special trucks have been designed to go where cars couldn't – on rocky terrain, up steep slopes or on snowy or muddy ground. Special tyres, special climbing gears and four-wheel drive provide traction.

Some of these features are now part of family cars called sports utility vehicles (SUVs). It's common for people to take these cars off-road into areas that were once too rugged for family cars. And engineering breakthroughs mean that cars might even double as boats or planes. The sky's the limit – or is it?

Some SUVs can climb slopes of 45 degrees – that means they're climbing the same distance that they're moving forward. The steepest street in the world measures only 19 degrees.

Submersible cars

Cars designed to float – called car boats – have been around since the 1950s. Engineers have taken things a step further, or deeper. Once the driver of a Rinspeed sQuba floods the waterproof cockpit, the car sinks underwater and can travel like a submarine. The driver and passengers breathe through scuba-like tubes.

In some places, people call on four-wheel drive vehicles to drive students home if weather conditions suddenly grow worse, making roads dangerous.

Four-wheel drive

The engines of most cars power movement in either the back axle (rear-wheel drive) or the front (front-wheel drive). Off-road vehicles have four-wheel drive, giving more secure traction on slippery or unstable surfaces. All-wheel drive (AWD) systems go further by sensing which wheels have a firmer grip – giving them more power and reducing power for wheels that aren't secure.

Can you believe it?

The Lunar Roving Vehicle, or 'moon buggy', was used on NASA's last three lunar missions in 1971 and 1972.

Going to extremes

Monster dump trucks

The biggest construction jobs – building dams, digging mines or blasting roads through mountains – call for the biggest, most powerful trucks on Earth. The largest uses an engine that packs about 4,000 horsepower!

Some of the most dramatic vehicles on or off the road are genuine giants. Whether they're super long, super heavy, or super powerful, they harness science to make the best use of their scale.

Hand in hand with size is power. Yet again, Newton's Laws of Motion help explain why. Just as it takes more strength (force) to throw a bowling ball compared to a tennis ball, it takes a much larger engine to power these giants of the road than it does to power the engine of your much smaller family car.

Most family cars have engines of about 150 horsepower... dwarfed by comparison with monster trucks.

Hey! It's my big brother!

Huge flatbed trucks carried 90 wind turbine blades, each more than 52 metres (172 feet) long, up a 2,900 metre (9,514 foot) mountain in China.

Stretch limo

Engineers need to 'think big' when they turn ordinary cars into eye-catching stretch limos. Several drivetrains are linked together to reach the rear axle, and electrical connectors ensure that power reaches the entire vehicle.

Moving house - literally!

Special trucks are designed to carry enormous loads, including entire houses!

Multiple axles are needed to spread the enormous mass of the payload.

Can you believe it?

Most big trucks have a tractor unit towing a large trailer. But the massive 'road trains' of Australia have three or more trailers towed by a single tractor unit. The longest-ever road train had 112 trailers stretching 1,474 metres (4,837 feet).

New Sources of power

Electric cars

Cars and trucks that run on electricity instead of petrol or diesel produce hardly any air pollution. Their engines are almost silent. That cuts down on noise pollution, but creates a problem of its own: how to warn pedestrians that a car is near them? There are plans to have these vehicles fitted with audible alert systems.

Internal combustion engines have powered cars and trucks for well over a century, but the world now faces a problem – we might run out of fuel. The petrol and diesel that make those engines run are produced from oil, and scientists can't agree on whether we will run out soon.

That's because oil is a fossil fuel, created over millions of years as plankton, or microscopic organisms, decay and become oil and natural gas. We're using up the fuel faster than it's being produced, so supplies aren't limitless. The race is on to build vehicles that will use less fossil fuels, or even use fuel that's produced from renewable sources.

Vehicle exhaust fumes are one of the worst contributors to global warming. They contain carbon dioxide gas, which collects in the Earth's atmosphere and acts like a blanket, heating the planet.

9

NO FUEL!

Hybrid vehicles

Some vehicles, called hybrids, use a mixture of petrol and electric power. They have two motors. At low speeds, the electric motor powers the car. When more power is needed – to accelerate quickly or to climb – the petrol motor takes over. But the electric motor also acts as a generator, storing electric power for when it's next needed.

Battery

Generator

Electric motor

Internal combustion engine

Power split device

The race is on to produce electric-car batteries that can be charged quickly and hold their charge for many hours. Charging stations, where people can recharge batteries, are becoming more common each year.

Hydrogen alternative

Hydrogen is being tested as a non-polluting alternative to fossil fuels, especially in heavy vehicles. Compressed hydrogen is converted to electricity to power the vehicle, and the only exhaust is water.

Fascinating facts

There are different ways of calculating how fuel-efficient a vehicle is. For internal-combustion engines, the UK, USA and some other countries work out how far (in miles) a gallon of petrol will let a car travel – miles per gallon (mpg). Other countries use a system based on how many litres of petrol are needed to travel 100 kilometres (L/100km).

It's not just trucks and cars that will be getting 'smarter' in the future: roads will also be linked to computer systems on trucks and cars. Information about roadworks, accidents or unusual weather conditions will be fed into car systems.

The future

Sometimes things that at first seem like problems can turn out to be inspiration for new inventions. For example, in recent decades, obstacles such as fossil fuels running out, overcrowding and pollution have helped spark the development of electric vehicles and cleaner fuels.

With driverless cars already in production, the world is preparing for even more dramatic developments. Just as smartphones and the Internet keep people connected full time, vehicles will be constantly sending and receiving information to make driving safer and faster.

Flying cars?

The idea of being able to hop into a car and then take off into the sky has been a fantasy for more than a century... but could it become a reality? The Terrafugia TF-X, still in the testing stage, is a flying car that can take off vertically and fly for up to 800 kilometres (500 miles) at a cruising speed of 320 kph (200 mph).

Kid's eye view

A British company asked children to design cars for the future. Some left science out of the picture to concentrate on dragon-shaped vehicles and cupcake boosters to add power, but some other ideas could pave the way for real developments. Vehicle designers are already considering some of the ideas that came up, like colour-changing materials and flexible glass for driving underwater.

Robot trucks will be able to carry passengers along fixed routes, like between airport terminals. Robot trucks are already carrying freight along highways in Arizona, stopping just before their destinations to let humans finish the drive.

'Calling all cars'

Tiny cars – which take up hardly any space and can be summoned by smartphone – could help solve parking problems and provide low-cost transport in the future.

How it works

A smartphone is really a computer as well as a communications device. And it combines the computing and communicating to work out exactly where it is, using GPS (like the SatNav in a car). When people call a mini-car, they're automatically telling the car where they are – so it can make its way to them.

Glossary

Aerodynamic Having a smooth, streamlined shape that reduces the effect of air resistance.

All-wheel drive An engine system (abbreviated as AWD) that provides power to wheels with good traction and reduces power to those with less traction.

Axle A shaft with turning wheels at each end.

Centre of mass The point, sometimes called centre of gravity, where all the mass of an object is concentrated.

Chassis The frame supporting the engine and body of a road vehicle.

Collision An event in which two or more moving objects crash together.

Compressed air Air that has been pumped into a container, and which is released with great force.

Crankshaft A long metal rod that helps the engine turn the wheels of a vehicle.

Cylinder A cylinder-shaped chamber housing a piston in an internal combustion engine.

Deluge gun A high-powered, aimable water jet that is used in firefighting.

Differential A rotating, angled gear that changes the direction of rotation in road vehicles.

Drivetrain The system that connects a motor vehicle's engine with the drive axle.

Energy The ability to do work.

Exhaust The waste gas given off by an engine during internal combustion.

Force The push or pull on an object when it meets another object.

Fossil fuel A fuel, such as oil, coal or natural gas that is produced over millions of years from the remains of living things.

Four-wheel drive An engine system that provides power to the front and rear axles, so that all four wheels are powered.

Friction The resistance of something to motion, often causing a moving object to slow down.

Fuel-efficient Able to produce power using relatively little fuel.

G-force A measure of force on an object, representing the amount of force that gravity has on that object.

Gearbox A set of gears, inside a casing, that provides the most efficient way of transferring energy from the engine to the wheels.

Global warming An overall increase in world temperature caused by a combination of natural actions, such as volcanic eruptions, and human-made effects, like the gases produced globally by powered vehicles.

GPS An abbreviation of Global Positioning System, a method of locating a position on Earth by communicating with satellites.

Impact The meeting of objects with great force.

Industrial Revolution A period in the eighteenth and nineteenth centuries when inventors and engineers developed new machines which used steam and other sources of power.

Internal combustion A system of providing power by burning a mixture of petrol (or other burnable fuel) and air inside an engine; the hot gases that are produced expand and drive pistons.

Mass The amount of matter in an object.

Newton's Laws of Motion A set of three basic laws, proposed by English scientist Isaac Newton, to describe how an object reacts to forces acting on it.

Torque The ability of a force to produce a twisting motion.

31

Index